Cash In On Strangers

How to get strangers to buy your stuff Over and over

James D. Hudson

Table of contents

Introduction

*Everyone is not your customer." – **Seth Godin***

A Marketer's Odyssey James D. Hudson once lived in Commerceville, a busy metropolis. James was no stranger to the pull of entrepreneurship; his ambitions were painted in the vivid hues of success, but his path was shadowed by a constant challenge—one that whispered doubts in the stillness of his undertakings.

James, like many other businesses, was faced with the onerous task of acquiring customers. The streets of Commerceville were teeming with potential consumers, but James found himself at a crossroads, unsure of which path would lead him to these elusive customers.

His adventure began with enthusiasm, a head full of ideas, and a heart filled with determination. But as he navigated the complicated alleyways of business, a harsh reality emerged: attracting new consumers was no easy task. Nights became thoughtful moments, and each day presented a new set of obstacles.

The first obstacle James faced was the notion that a large number of leads would immediately convert into success. However, as he gathered more leads, it became clear that quantity did not equate to quality connections. James saw that each lead was an individual with a distinct story, desires, and obstacles.

This insight signaled the commencement of a new chapter in James's entrepreneurial path. He saw that in order to make real relationships, he needed to move beyond generic techniques. Thus, the notion of "Cash In On Strangers" was born—a strategy that viewed each potential client as an individual with a story to tell.

The essence of the problem lay not in getting leads but in grasping them. James set out on a quest to engage potential clients authentically. It was no longer enough to just provide a product or service; instead, it was necessary to create an irresistible attraction through carefully constructed offers and lead magnets.

As James delved deeper into the domain of comprehension, he discovered warm outreach—a genuine attempt to engage with potential clients on a more human basis. He realized that effective communication is more than just a transaction; it is the start of a conversation.

But the journey didn't end there. James faced the difficulty of reaching out to others who had yet to hear his tale. Cold outreach became the next frontier—a daring attempt to say "hello" in a crowded gathering and lend a hand of introduction to those unfamiliar with his story.

The digital landscape attracted James with its huge potential, and James ventured into the realm of advertising. He discovered a canvas on which to paint his digital tale, hoping that each ad would evoke the honesty and passion that constituted his brand.

However, the story grew beyond the individual efforts. James recognized the value of obtaining lead producers. Referrals transformed into allies—clients who not only believed in James' narrative but actively shared it with others.

Employees became ambassadors, spreading the brand's message through their networks. Collaboration with external forces proved to be a game-changer. Affiliate programs and agencies were crucial allies, spreading James' message across larger landscapes.

The understanding struck: marketing was not limited to digital environments. "Advertising in Real Life" became a catchphrase, a reminder that the story needed to be heard beyond screens, reaching potential customers where they lived, worked, and played.

As James reflects on these stages in his entrepreneurial journey, he understands that the key to traversing the commercial frontier is to understand, engage sincerely, and enlist supporters.

As a result, "Cash In On Strangers" is more than simply a book; it's a handbook based on James' experiences and successes.

In the next chapters, James, your storyteller and guide, will reveal the techniques that shaped his journey.

He asks you, other entrepreneurs and adventurers, to join him on this journey. Together, you will discover the power of warm outreach, cold outreach, running advertising, and the art of recruiting even more new clients via recommendations, employees, affiliate programs, and agencies.

So get ready for the developing story—a tale of difficulties, successes, and the essence of becoming true Cash In On Strangers. The trip continues, and with each turn of the page, you push deeper into the corporate frontier, ready to face the difficulties that await

Chapter 1: Let Us Begin

"The secret to getting ahead is getting started."
Mark Twain

In the heart of Commerceville, where the sun painted the sky with hues of possibilities, James D. Hudson stood on the verge of his entrepreneurial journey. The air was filled with expectancy, and the city's cadence echoed his exhilaration.

James, a believer with a burning heart, was about to go on a trip that would intertwine his fate with the fabric of Commerceville's bustling streets. The story unfolded in James' humble office, which he referred to as his beginning point—a refuge of dreams where ideas flourished and goals took their first breaths.

The walls, covered with motivating slogans and sketches of future ideas, told stories of individuals who had dared to dream before him. As James sat in the controlled chaos of his creative area, recollections of the journey's beginning flooded his thoughts. It all started with a spark—a flash of inspiration that fueled the urge to create something worthwhile. The concept, like a little seed, grew into a vision that went beyond the bounds of conventional dreams.

The city, with its winding lanes, awaited James's arrival. He envisioned a business that was not constrained by conventional conventions but rather resonated with the pounding pulse of Commerceville—one that would not only succeed but also contribute to the community's tapestry.

The day of reckoning arrived when James made that decisive move—the opening of his storefront. The "Cash In On Strangers" sign was proudly displayed, alerting the world that a new player had entered the arena.

It was a modest start, but behind the surface, a stream of energy flowed—a resolve to unravel the mysteries of marketing and construct a distinct narrative. The first few days were a blur of introductions, handshakes, and the wonderful scent of expectation.

As the doorbell rang with each entry, James understood he wasn't just establishing a business; he was starting a conversation with Commerceville—a conversation interlaced with marketing, narrative, and common goals.

The early hurdles arrived, as they typically do in the early stages of any entrepreneur's narrative. James came face-to-face with the conundrum of customer acquisition. Despite the bustling pace of commerce, the streets appeared to preserve potential clients' secrets like ancient gatekeepers.

The challenge was clear: how can you cut through the noise, stand out from the crowd, and connect with individuals who are concealed in Commerceville's huge landscape? This question lingered, not as an impediment but as an invitation to go on a journey of understanding and discovery.

James would sit in the peaceful minutes after the closing hours, surrounded by the echoes of the day's events. During these contemplative pauses, the concept of "Cash In On Strangers" began to take shape—a philosophy that saw each potential client as an undiscovered story waiting to be told.

The route, despite its uncertainty, became an odyssey of engagement. It was no longer enough to provide a product or service; it was also necessary to create an experience that spoke to the hearts and minds of individuals who entered the store.

As the days moved into weeks and weeks into months, James recognized that he was not alone on this adventure. His clients were more than just transactions; they were characters in a drama that changed with each passing day.

The storefront became a stage, and each encounter added a new chapter to the story of the "Cash In On Strangers." And as the first chapter of James D. Hudson's entrepreneurial story unfolded, it became evident that this was more than just a business; it was an expedition. An odyssey of ambitions realized, problems transformed into possibilities, and a journey as dynamic and unexpected as Commerceville itself. The setting was set, the characters were presented, and the story had only just begun.

Solving Large Problems

"If I had an hour to solve a problem I'd spend 55 minutes thinking about the problem and 5 minutes thinking about solutions."
Albert Einstein

In the city where James established his business, he saw that many people experienced significant challenges when attempting to make their businesses successful. The first major issue was attracting new clients.

It was like attempting to uncover buried treasure in a crowded area. James wanted to assist individuals understand and interact with consumers, not just as numbers, but as actual people with unique stories.

He learned that speaking politely to potential consumers, reaching out in various ways, and delivering a good story might make a tremendous difference. So his book, "Cash In On Strangers," will teach entrepreneurs these innovative techniques to communicate and engage with others.

However, that was not the only issue. James understood the importance of discovering new clients in a variety of ways, such as asking friends for aid, involving the team, or collaborating with others.

This book aimed to function as a map, demonstrating how to navigate these various roads and attract even more people interested in what you have to offer. Real-world advertising presented another puzzle to solve. James believed that it was more than just putting stuff on the internet; it was also about telling your narrative in real life.

The book would include suggestions for how to do this, making your story visible where people live and work. Putting all of these principles together may appear complicated, but the book sought to make it simple.

It served as a guide, demonstrating how friendly conversations might complement advertisements or how seeking assistance from friends could coexist with approaching others outside of your business.

The idea was for everything to fit together nicely, like jigsaw pieces. The book was about more than simply methods; it was also about maintaining a cool attitude. James wanted entrepreneurs to think outside the box, to be creative, and to avoid doing things the same way.

He believed that telling a good tale had the potential to transform difficult situations into exciting opportunities. Collaboration, such as working with friends or special groups, became a major theme in the novel. These weren't just assistants; they were like teammates.

The book described how having these colleagues would make the journey easier and more enjoyable. As James examined the difficulties his book was addressing, he noticed a story unfolding.

It wasn't just about the struggles; it was about overcoming obstacles and providing entrepreneurs with the necessary tools to navigate the fascinating world of business.

The book was like a buddy, providing answers, motivation, and the promise that difficult times could be turned into steps toward success in the huge and fascinating world of business.

Chapter 2: Understanding the Tale of Your Clients

"Your most unhappy customers are your greatest source of learning."
Bill Gates

In the heart of Commerceville, where the rhythm of business played a vibrant melody, James D. Hudson embarked on a quest to unravel a crucial lesson: finding new clients was not merely about numbers but about understanding the unique tales they carried.

The journey began one bustling morning as James opened the doors to "Cash In On Strangers." The storefront, a hub of dreams and aspirations, welcomed a steady flow of visitors. Yet James sensed there was more to this dance of commerce than meets the eye.

As he engaged with the steady stream of potential clients, a realization crystallized—each person walking through the door brought with them a story, a narrative waiting to be heard.

It was not enough to see them as faceless numbers on a spreadsheet; to truly connect, one needed to understand the individual chapters that shaped their journey.

The first lesson unfolded in a simple conversation with Emily, a small business owner seeking marketing guidance. As she shared her challenges and aspirations, James listened not just with his ears but with a genuine curiosity to comprehend her story.

Emily's journey wasn't just about numbers or transactions; it was about her passion, struggles, and dreams for her business. James discovered that understanding went beyond the surface—beyond what products or services clients sought.

It delved into the motivations, fears, and desires that fueled their entrepreneurial spirit. Each person was a protagonist in their own narrative, and to connect authentically, James needed to become not just a marketer but a storyteller, attuned to the nuances of each individual plot.

As the days turned into weeks, James met a variety of characters in the grand story of "Cash In On Strangers." There was Mike, the young entrepreneur with a tech startup, driven by a desire to innovate. And there was Sarah, a seasoned business owner with a family legacy to uphold.

Each encounter became an opportunity to understand their unique challenges, aspirations, and the chapters they wished to script in the tale of their businesses.

To illustrate the importance of understanding, James crafted personalized strategies for each client. It wasn't a one-size-fits-all approach but a tailored narrative that resonated with the essence of their story.

For Mike, it was about highlighting innovation and cutting-edge solutions; for Sarah, it was about honoring tradition while embracing modernity. In the heart of this journey, James encountered Mark, a restaurateur facing the challenge of standing out in a saturated market.

Instead of bombarding him with generic marketing tactics, James sat down with Mark, seeking to unravel the nuances of his culinary narrative. The solution wasn't just about advertising the menu but capturing the essence of Mark's culinary passion and the unique flavors that defined his restaurant.

James's realization expanded beyond the walls of his storefront. It became a guiding principle, a beacon that illuminated the path for entrepreneurs. The essence was clear: finding new clients wasn't a transactional game—it was a journey into the stories that shaped them.

Each person had a narrative, and understanding that narrative was the key to forging meaningful connections. The lessons continued to unfold, each client bringing a new chapter to the evolving narrative of "Cash In On Strangers."

The storefront became a tapestry of diverse stories, a testament to the power of understanding in the world of business. As

James reflected on this chapter of his entrepreneurial saga, he understood that the journey of "Cash In On Strangers" wasn't just about finding new clients; it was about weaving a tapestry of connections, understanding the tales of those who walked through the door, and becoming a storyteller who spoke the language of each individual narrative.

The storefront wasn't just a place of transactions; it was a space where stories converged and where, with every engagement, a new chapter unfolded in the grand tale of Commerce Ville.

Creating Tales of Delight: Offers and Lead Magnets

"People don't buy for logical reasons. They buy for emotional reasons." – **Zig Ziglar**

In the heart of Commerceville, where the art of business waltzed with creativity, James D. Hudson discovered a vital truth: creating clients was more than just transactions; it was about constructing stories of delight through compelling offers and captivating lead magnets.

The revelation occurred on a day that had the promise of a new story. As James sipped his morning coffee, he wondered how to give the "Cash In On Strangers" boutique a unique attraction.

In order to create a really captivating experience, he focused on the concept of offers and lead magnets. The adventure began with the creation of an attractive offer—a narrative hook that would draw potential clients into the realm of "Cash In On Strangers."

It was more than just a discount or a promotional gimmick; it was an expression of gratitude to those who chose to be a part of this evolving story. James realized that a compelling offer was more than simply its financial value; it was also about the story it conveyed.

It was an invitation, a start to a relationship between the company and the customer. So he came up with an offer that appealed to the soul of his brand: a discount for early explorers, a sign of shared excitement for the voyage ahead. As the offer progressed, the response was instantaneous.

The storefront hummed with activity as potential customers, tempted by the promise of a special welcome, entered the realm of "Cash In On Strangers." The offer was more than just a transaction; it was the start of a debate that extended beyond figures and charts.

However, the story did not finish with the offer; it only laid the groundwork for a more complex narrative—the domain of lead magnets. James realized that to genuinely capture the audience, he needed to deliver something of worth, something that would improve their own tales.

As a result, lead magnets were created: appealing morsels of knowledge, tools, or experiences that future clients couldn't pass up. It wasn't about pushing a product or service; it was about giving them a taste of the brand's essence, a glimpse of the adventure that lay ahead.

A downloaded handbook on unique marketing methods served as a lead magnet for the tech-savvy entrepreneur researching "Cash In On Strangers." It was more than simply a document; it was a wealth of knowledge, a compass directing them through the difficulties of the corporate frontier.

Sarah, the experienced business owner, was piqued by a webinar invitation about the merging of tradition and modernity in marketing.

The lead magnet was more than just a webinar; it was a fully immersive experience, a virtual adventure that promised to educate and inspire.

As potential clients interacted with these lead magnets, a story of reciprocity emerged.

It was not a one-sided transaction; rather, it was an exchange of value. Clients received not just a discount but also knowledge, insights, and a glimpse into the unique methodology of "Cash In On Strangers." The magic occurred when these contributions were smoothly incorporated into the ongoing story.

The offer acted as a prologue, the lead magnet as the first chapter, and the unfolding adventure as the story center. It was more than just collecting clients; it was about creating a community—a fellowship of adventurers united by shared passion and stories.

The success of the deals and lead magnets was assessed not only by numbers but also by the conversations, connections, and tales that echoed throughout the storefront. Clients were more than simply customers; they were protagonists in a story of exploration and discovery.

As James thought about this chapter in his entrepreneurial journey, he realized the value of telling stories of delight. The storefront was more than just a venue for transactions; it was a theater where offers and lead magnets played out as scenarios, adding to a story that stretched well beyond Commerceville's borders.

It was a reminder that, in the world of "Cash In On Strangers," acquiring clients was more than just a business transaction; it was a storytelling endeavor—a narrative crafted with offers that sparkled like gems and lead magnets that unfolded like chapters, inviting clients to become co-authors in the ongoing journey.

Chapter 3: Conversations That Echo: Different Ways to Communicate with New Clients

*"If you can't explain it simply, you don't understand it well enough." —**Albert Einstein***

In the vibrant center of Commerceville, where every street hummed with the hum of possibilities, James D. Hudson set out on a journey to discover the art of conversation—different ways to communicate with new clients that went beyond conventional transactions.

As the sun painted the sky with colors of anticipation, James contemplated the various stories that awaited discovery. He realized that getting new clients was more than just creating noise; it was about striking chords with each potential client's unique story.

The initial line of inquiry was friendly outreach, a kind strategy that aimed to engage new clients in meaningful talks. James saw this as more than just an introduction; it was an invitation, a warm handshake that moved beyond the transactional and into the personal.

One morning, as sunlight flooded through the windows of "Cash In On Strangers," James made a warm outreach to Emily, a budding entrepreneur seeking advice.

Instead of hammering her with sales pitches, he sat down for a casual conversation, learning about not only her business needs but also the hopes and objectives that drove her entrepreneurial spirit.

The warmth of the talk fostered a relationship that extended beyond the immediate transaction. Emily, feeling understood and valued, became a participant in the ongoing story of "Cash In On Strangers."

Warm outreach, James recognized, was more than just a plan; it was the skill of building relationships. However, the tale went beyond warmth and embraced the cool breeze of cold outreach.

James saw that some potential consumers were like distant stars, waiting to be discovered in the wide expanse of Commerce Ville. Cold outreach was not about intruding; rather, it was about sending a kind wave in the crowded cosmic dance of business.

James approached businesses that hadn't yet become "Cash In On Strangers" with elegance. Rather than bombarding them with generic messages, he created bespoke invitations that were suited to the recipient's individual characteristics.

The goal was not only to introduce the brand but also to spark a conversation—a cool breeze whispering stories about what "Cash In On Strangers" had to offer. The internet landscape became a canvas for another type of conversation: running advertisements.

These advertisements, according to James, were not interruptions but rather storylines that could captivate attention and pique curiosity. He created each advertisement as a piece of a larger story, allowing potential clients to enter the world of "Cash In On Strangers" and become characters in their own business stories.

James saw the ripple effect as the advertisements moved across the screen. They were more than just advertisements; they were calls to adventure, inviting potential clients to join the story and explore the unknown frontiers of creative marketing.

The storytelling did not stop there; it continued into the world of lead generation. James saw that in order to magnify the narrative, he needed allies—characters in the story that could advocate "Cash In On Strangers."

Referrals, the first chapter in this part, began as clients became storytellers, sharing their great experiences and urging others to join the journey.

In the case of employee advocacy, the team became narrators, disseminating the brand's story through their networks. The affiliate program became a collaborative chapter, inviting external allies to become part of the broader plot.

Each lead generation approach was more than a transactional tool; it was a tale in and of itself. Referral stories described delighted clients evolving into ardent champions, creating a tapestry of trust and confidence.

Employee advocacy stories emerged as team members became ambassadors, injecting authenticity into the brand's story.

The affiliate program narrative expanded beyond company partnerships, becoming a saga of external allies banding together, giving varied viewpoints to the main story of "Cash In On Strangers."

And so, in the heart of Commerceville, the many techniques to approach new clients were more than simply strategies; they were chapters in an ongoing story. Warm outreach, cold outreach, running advertising, recommendations, workers, and external allies were not separate parts but rather threads in the rich tapestry of "Cash In On Strangers."

As James thought on this stage of his entrepreneurial journey, he realized that the art of conversation was more than just exchanging words; it was the harmony of several voices adding to a symphony of connection and understanding.

The storefront was more than simply a place to shop; it was a stage where tales intersected and conversations echoed—a testimonial to the many ways in which "Cash In On Strangers" communicated to the hearts and minds of all who entered its embrace.

The Elegance of Warm Outreach: Communicating Nicely with New Clients

"The most difficult thing is the decision to act. The rest is merely tenacity." —**Amelia Earhart**

In the heart of Commerceville, where the pulse of possibility reverberated through the streets, James D. Hudson set out to investigate the art of conversation through the lens of warmth—a journey into the realm of warm outreach, where speaking nicely to new clients was more than a strategy, but an eloquent dance of connection.

As dawn painted the sky in shades of anticipation, James found himself reflecting on the intricacies of actual engagement. He saw warm outreach as more than just a business strategy; it was a gesture, an extension of hospitality that drew potential clients into the welcome arms of "Cash In On Strangers."

The unfolding story began one sunny afternoon when Emily, a determined businesswoman, entered the storefront seeking advice. Rather than hitting her with an immediate sales pitch, James used a different approach. He invited her to a pleasant corner, giving not only a seat but also an opportunity for serious conversation.

The essence of friendly outreach was to create an environment in which potential clients felt cherished and understood. James spoke without a script, but with genuine interest, while Emily revealed the ambitions and obstacles that fuelled her business spirit.

The atmosphere became a canvas for connection—an interaction that extended beyond business. James didn't just ask about company needs; he wanted to know Emily's story, the chapters that defined her path. Warm outreach, he concluded, was not a one-size-fits-all attempt;

it was about personalizing the conversation to the distinct melody of each person's experience.

As James began his exploration, he met Mike, a tech innovator who is passionate about pushing the boundaries. The encounter unfolded as a dialogue rather than a sales pitch, with James listening to Mike's aspirations, celebrating his triumphs, and genuinely engaging with the narrative of his IT career.

The power of friendly outreach lay not just in the knowledge shared, but also in the emotional resonance it generated. Potential clients became more than just bystanders in the unfolding drama of "Cash In On Strangers."

James spoke with the subtlety of a storyteller, making connections that went deeper than the surface.

Sarah, a seasoned business owner with a legacy to honor, joined the story of welcoming outreach. James, knowing the significance of her experience, did not approach her with a standard pitch. Instead, he engaged in a conversation that celebrated her journey, honoring the various chapters of her business story and demonstrating how "Cash In On Strangers" could contribute to the ongoing story.

The elegance of welcoming outreach stretched beyond the storefront. James investigated the digital landscape, where emails became letters and phone calls became conversations. It was more than just delivering a message; it was also about creating a discussion that struck a chord with the recipient.

As James navigated these interactions, he realized that warmth was more than simply a transient impression; it was the cornerstone of long-term partnerships.

It wasn't about rushing to the sale; it was about planting seeds of understanding and cultivating long-term relationships.

In the big symphony of friendly outreach, each possible client became a note—a distinct melody that added to the harmonious composition of "Cash In On Strangers." The shop wasn't just a site of transactions; it was a stage where the art of speaking politely transcended the mundane and became a performance of connection and honesty.

As the sun set on another day in Commerceville, James reflected on the beauty of warm outreach. It wasn't just a plan; it was a philosophy—a concept that in the business world, speaking politely was more than a courtesy; it was the key to opening the doors of genuine connection and forging relationships that would echo throughout the chapters of "Cash In On Strangers."

The storefront, now bathed in the mellow glow of evening, stood as a tribute to the elegance of friendly outreach—a place where discussions resonated and potential customers became more than simply patrons, but beloved participants in the unfolding story.

The Cool Connection: Reaching Out and Sharing Awesome Stuff

*Only by giving are you able to receive more than you already have." **Jim Rohn***

In the vibrant hub of Commerceville, where possibilities abound, James D. Hudson chose to take a chilly but friendly approach: reach out to new acquaintances with cold outreach and show them great goods through advertising.

Imagine you're in a vast metropolis with many enterprises, like lights flashing in the night sky. James intended to greet these distant stars with a kind gesture, rather than being forceful.

He dubbed it "cold outreach." His canvas for this voyage was the internet world, where advertisements transformed into intriguing stories waiting to be uncovered.

Instead of assaulting these distant stars with monotonous messages, James created personalized invitations. Every ad provided a sneak glimpse at what "Cash In On Strangers" had to offer.

It was more than just providing services; it was also about presenting stories that piqued people's interest.

Mike, a tech guru who enjoyed experimenting with new technologies, was one of these distant stars. James used advertising language to illustrate the inventive tactics and cool solutions that "Cash In On Strangers" could provide.

The commercial was more than just a blip on the screen; it seemed like the start of an exciting story, asking Mike to be the hero of his professional journey.

Cold outreach was not about being remote; it was about generating interest. The advertisements were more than just product information; they were visual stories that sparked the imagination.

Instead of being a passive observer, potential clients became active participants, clicking and asking questions, thereby entering the exciting world of possibility.

Cold outreach was flexible. James saw that different firms had unique great stories to share. Sarah, a seasoned business owner striving for balance, saw the ad as more than a pitch; it was a visual feast.

It featured cool concepts and modern ways that aligned with Sarah's ambition to combine tradition with innovation.

Cold outreach worked not only to grab notice, but also to pique people's interest. Every click and inquiry was a step into the cool world of "Cash In On Strangers," transforming the coldness of outreach into warm involvement.

The coolness of outreach extended beyond the digital realm. James also looked into real-world advertising. Billboards, brochures, and events became platforms for telling tales, enabling potential customers to interact with the business in tangible ways.

James discovered that the key to successful cold outreach was not just the advertising itself, but also the tale it communicated. The cool innovations were more than just services; they were like chapters in a tale, each intended to make the business trip more fascinating for potential clients.

As the stars twinkled in Commerceville's night sky, James admired the chilly artistry of cold outreach. It wasn't about breaking down walls; it was about sending a pleasant wave, allowing potential clients to explore the cool landscapes of commercial opportunities.

The shop, now lighting in the night, served as testimony of the cool stories told through frigid outreach. Each ad was more than just a digital blip; it was a stroke on the canvas of "Cash In On Strangers."

The Arctic winds of outreach, formerly thought to be remote and chilly, have transformed into a soft breeze, whispering stories of fascinating creations and asking potential clients to join the journey of exploration and discovery.

Connecting in Special Ways: Simple and Effective Methods to Reach Out

*Approach each customer with the idea of helping him or her solve a problem or achieve a goal, not of selling a product or service." — **Brian Tracy.***

In the midst of bustling Commerceville, where business tunes played, James D. Hudson investigated easy and efficient ways to engage with potential clients.

Each method, he believed, was more than just a plan, but a distinct tool in the orchestra of connection, playing its own simple and useful tune.

As the sun set, painting the city in warm hues, James reflected on the simplicity of warm outreach—the opening note in this orchestra.

He recalled a conversation with Emily, an enthusiastic entrepreneur seeking advice. Warm outreach was like a pleasant hug, making potential clients feel appreciated.

Warm outreach was not about selling, but about developing relationships. When James sat down with Emily, he listened not only with his ears, but with genuine curiosity, grasping her goals and challenges.

The unique tune of warm outreach was not a sales pitch, but rather the art of making connections.

The next note in the orchestra was cold outreach, which produced a distinctive sound. James considered reaching out to businesses like stars in the vast universe of Commerceville.

Cold outreach felt like a welcoming wave, an invitation to discover the exciting possibilities that "Cash In On Strangers" had to offer.

Creating individualized invites was the key. Each advertisement provided a glimpse into the cool world of the corporation. Cold outreach was about more than simply attracting notice; it was also about piqueing potential clients' interest and converting them into active participants.

Then came the running ads—a vibrant note dancing across screens and billboards. James saw that advertisements were not interruptions, but rather pieces of a broader story, allowing potential clients to enter the realm of "Cash In On Strangers."

The unique melody of running commercials was more than just promotion; it was about creating an immersive experience.

Advertisements evolved into visual storytelling that painted a narrative of possibilities rather than simply showcasing services.

The distinct melody of running advertising was not just about selling; it was also about providing an experience that spoke to each potential client's specific goals.

The story expanded into the realm of lead getters, with a chapter featuring several harmonies. Referrals were the first thing mentioned, as delighted customers converted into enthusiastic storytellers.

James recalled how clients such as Mike and Sarah became ambassadors, sharing their positive experiences and urging others to join the journey.

Employee advocacy was another thriving harmony. The crew did more than just participate; they became narrators, promoting the brand's message throughout their networks.

The affiliate program offered an external ally, resulting in a collaborative chapter in which several points of view worked together to tell the larger story.

Each lead generation approach was more than simply a transactional tool; it was a distinctive symphony that added to the rich tapestry of "Cash In On Strangers." The unique melody of lead getters was about more than simply acquiring clients; it was about creating a community—a fellowship of explorers united by shared passion and tales.

The orchestra's last piece was advertising in real life, a big crescendo that rang beyond computer screens. James realized the value of concrete experiences, and real-world channels became platforms for showcasing cool ideas.

Billboards, fliers, and events were more than simply physical things; they were extensions of the brand's story, asking potential customers to participate in real ways.

The roadmap evolved as the grand conclusion, a song that brought all of these distinct sounds together. James envisioned a comprehensive approach in which warm and cold outreach, running commercials, lead generation, and real-life advertising all worked together fluidly.
It wasn't just about individual methods; it was about creating a full story that led potential clients on the voyage of "Cash In On Strangers."

As James considered the orchestra of connection, he understood that each path was not simply a tool, but a distinct instrument, adding its own tune to the overall composition.

The shop, now illuminated by the soft light of twilight, stood as a tribute to the various and harmonious ways "Cash In On Strangers" interacted with potential clients.

In the vast orchestra of business, James had realized that each method—warm outreach, cold outreach, running commercials, lead generators, and real-life advertising—played a unique and valuable function.

Together, they created a melodic narrative, asking potential clients to join the journey and become important components of the ever-changing story of "Cash In On Strangers."

Chapter 4: Attracting More New Clients: A Journey to Growth

*Customer service is important even before the ideal client has paid you. They'll never forget you for understanding them- **James D. Hudson***

In the bustling town of Commerceville, where business stories unfolded, James D. Hudson considered the search for new clients for his company, "Cash In On Strangers."

James tried a variety of strategies to expand his clientele and make them feel like they were a part of the fascinating journey.

The first approach he used was to practice "Referral Magic." James realized that his current clients were storytellers who could share the excitement of their journey with "Cash In On Strangers."

He encouraged them to bring in new clients and extended a warm invitation to join the voyage. As Mike, a computer enthusiast, shared his positive experiences with others, the customer base grew, with each new addition becoming an important character in the evolving plot.
The hunt then switched to the theme of "Employee Teamwork." James realized that his

team was more than just a group of coworkers; it was like a family working together to achieve a common goal.

Encouraged his team to spread the word about the amazing things "Cash In On Strangers" could do, resulting in a workplace that felt like a huge family.

Each team member helped to make the organization more than just a service provider; it was also a community where consumers felt connected and valued.

The journey was expanded with the advent of "Ally Alliance" through the affiliate program. James saw external partners joining forces, contributing a diversity of knowledge and perspectives to strengthen the overall tale of "Cash In On Strangers."

These allies were more than just coworkers; they were friends, each adding their own chapter to the larger story. The affiliate program connected the company to a bigger network of clients, all of whom contributed to the growing story.

As the quest advanced, James researched the concept of "Agency Assistance." These were professional allies who specialized in specific tasks and volunteered their skills to enhance the client experience.

Whether through specialized services or strategic collaboration, these companies become crucial players in the growing tale of "Cash In On Strangers," lending their knowledge to the story.

When James studied each strategy, he recognized that obtaining new clients was more than just increasing numbers; it was also about building a dynamic community.

Referral Magic turned clients into storytellers, Employee Teamwork made the workplace feel more like a family, Ally Alliance widened the circle of friends, and Agency Assistance brought in professional partners.

In the heart of Commerceville, the circle of clients encircling "Cash In On Strangers" developed, becoming a community in which each client was more than a transaction; they were players in a tale.

The need to gain new clients turned into a voyage of connection and extension, resulting in a tapestry of relationships that defined the essence of "Cash In On Strangers."

So, in the bustling town where business stories unfolded, James D. Hudson embraced the ongoing quest to attract more new clients, realizing that the true magic lay not only in the strategies but also in the community they collectively built—an ever-expanding circle of clients, each playing a unique role in the exciting adventure of "Cash In On Strangers."

Clients Sharing Their Excitement: How They Spread the Word

Customers don't care at all whether you close the deal or not. They care about improving their business." —
Aaron Ross.

In the busy town of Commerceville, James D. Hudson developed a unique technique to increase the number of clients for "Cash In On Strangers." It was similar to a magical technique known as "referral."

Instead of James doing all the talking, he asked satisfied customers to share their experiences with other customers.

One day, James met a satisfied client named Mark. Mark was impressed with what "Cash In On Strangers" achieved for his firm.

James reasoned, "Why not ask Mark to tell his fellow clients about us?" So, he did exactly that.

He said, "Mark, you're our storyteller.

Share your experiences with other clients and tell them about your wonderful trip with us."

Mark enthusiastically agreed. He told his other clients about the unique techniques, successful initiatives, and how he had a genuine connection with the "Cash In On Strangers."

His fellow patrons became intrigued and decided to join in on the trip. When Mark's other customers became new clients, they shared their own stories and experiences.

The concept was like a friendly wave sweeping around town—a ripple effect of clients sharing their enthusiasm for "Cash In On Strangers."

The beauty of referral was more than just saying, "Hey, you should try this!" It was about the clients becoming storytellers. When clients shared their experiences, it felt authentic and trustworthy.

It was as if a fellow client had recommended a beloved movie or a cool spot to visit.

The ripple effect kept going. One client's referral prompted another, resulting in a chain reaction of clients joining the adventure.

The streets were alive with chatter about the incredible experiences clients had, attracting more curious people among their fellow clients who were eager to join the trip.

As the collection of clients grew, each new client offered something unique to the story. James grinned, realizing that the power of referrals was more than just acquiring new clients; it was also about creating a community of fellow clients who shared real tales and genuine recommendations.

James continued to promote the power of referrals in Commerceville, where words conveyed trust.

Clients sharing their delight became the lifeblood of "Cash In On Strangers," resulting in a web of stories that seemed genuine and enthusiastic.

So, in the ongoing adventure of business, James valued the power of clients sharing their excitement, knowing that this simple trick had turned into a welcoming melody—a tune that resonated across town, enticing new clients to join the vibrant story of "Cash In On Strangers."

Teamwork Tales: Employees As Ambassadors

*Talent wins games, but teamwork and intelligence win championships." – **Michael Jordan***

In the thriving town of Commerceville, where business stories thrived, James D. Hudson devised a great scheme to increase the number of clients for "Cash In On Strangers." He believed in the power of collaboration and considered his employees as vital partners in the company's expansion.

James assembled his team to convey his vision. "We're more than simply a bunch of people working together; we're like a large family on an exciting adventure. Let's tell our relatives and friends about all of our exciting activities."

His staff were thrilled by the camaraderie and agreed to become ambassadors for "Cash In On Strangers." They recognized that their voices had weight in their networks, and by sharing their positive experiences, they could attract more clients.

Emily, one of the team members, chatted with her cousin, who is beginning a small business. She discussed how the encouraging environment at "Cash In On Strangers" fostered creativity and achievement. Intrigued, her cousin decided to give it a shot, becoming a new customer and contributing a new chapter to the unfolding narrative.

Mike, another employee, spoke with a friend who owns a technology firm. He emphasized the innovative tactics and tailored approach of "Cash In On Strangers."

The friend was impressed by Mike's recommendation and joined the ranks of clients, adding his unique perspective to the ever-growing story.

Employees became ambassadors, and the workplace evolved into more than just an office. It became a forum for sharing excitement and stories.

These employee recommendations had a far-reaching impact, touching the lives of relatives and friends who, in turn, became a member of the vibrant community surrounding "Cash In On Strangers."

James admired the elegance of this collaboration story. It wasn't just about gaining more clients; it was about transforming employees into storytellers, creating authentic storylines.

The office buzzed with pride, knowing that they were not only providing services but also enticing others to join a booming clientele.

In the heart of Commerceville, where family and friendship were important, James continued to promote employee teamwork stories as ambassadors.

Employees became not just contributors but also narrators of the business story, creating an environment in which each recommendation became a thread in the bright tapestry of "Cash In On Strangers."

As the chapter progressed, it demonstrated the importance of enlisting the aid of family members, transforming employees into ambassadors whose tales strengthened the narrative and brought in more clients.

The voyage of growth continues, fueled by the genuine passion and shared stories of the dedicated staff at "Cash In On Strangers."

Allies in Adventure: The Affiliate Expedition

*Someone's sitting in the shade today because someone planted a tree a long time ago." – **Warren Buffett***

In the bustling town of Commerceville, James D. Hudson looked for fresh opportunities to bring in additional clients for "Cash In On Strangers."

The spirit of teamwork expanded beyond the office, inspiring him to create an alliance with external partners through the Affiliate Program—a strategy that turned clients into collaborators.

James set out to establish an opening for foreign allies to collaborate. He launched the Affiliate

Program, enabling individuals and organizations to join forces in the thrilling voyage of "Cash In On Strangers."

These external allies, known as affiliates, would be more than just clients; they would be active participants, each bringing their own perspective to the table.

As the training began, Emily, an entrepreneur, saw opportunities for collaboration. She became an affiliate and began promoting "Cash In On Strangers" to her network.

Her recommendations were more than just endorsements; they were invitations to investigate the company's innovative tactics and creative solutions.

Mike, another associate, ran a web development company. He recognized the importance of "Cash In On Strangers'" tailored approach and suggested their services to his clients.

The cooperation expanded beyond a simple referral to a partnership in which varied expertise fused to produce a fuller narrative for clients.

The Affiliate Program created a far-reaching ripple effect. Each affiliate contributed their unique spin to the overall story, presenting "Cash In On Strangers" to new audiences.

Clients became champions as a result of the collaborative atmosphere, and the narrative grew beyond individual experiences to include a common path of exploration and progress.

James admired the synergy formed by these foreign allies. It wasn't only about obtaining more clients; it was also about creating a network of partners who helped shape the ever-changing story of "Cash In On Strangers."

The affiliate program served as a bridge between different stories, resulting in a vibrant community united by a shared love for adventure.

James kept the Affiliate Expedition alive in the heart of Commerceville, where the spirit of collaboration thrived. The external allies, who are no longer just clients but active contributors, added layers to the narrative, transforming the business story into a mosaic of various experiences.

As a result, the chapter unfolded—a story of adventurers banding together through the Affiliate Program, transforming clients into collaborators.

The path of expansion continues, powered by the shared excitement and collaborative efforts of a growing community, linked by the common thread of "Cash In On Strangers."

Teamwork Triumphs: Accepting Agency Allies

The best marketing strategy of all times – "Care." –
Gary Vaynerchuk

In Commerceville, where James D. Hudson's "Cash In On Strangers" shared their company stories, a new chapter emerged—one that praised the power of collaboration in getting new clients.

Recognizing the importance of various knowledge, James sought the support of particular groups, forming alliances with agencies to increase the impact of his firm.

Approaching agencies with various capabilities, James envisioned a united front to expand the narrative of "Cash In On Strangers." Each agency provided their own unique perspective to the collective story.

A graphic design firm added visual appeal to the storyline, producing eye-catching pictures that grabbed potential clients.

Another digital marketing agency strategically promoted the exploits of "Cash In On Strangers" over the broad internet terrain. Collaborations included agencies specializing in content generation, event management, and other areas.

As these connections grew stronger, the favorable benefits of customer acquisition became more apparent. The relationship with agencies was more than just adding clients; it was a deliberate decision to improve the whole client experience, with each agency playing an important role.

James was impressed by the diverse group's collective impact. Beyond the goal of acquiring new clients, the collaborations with agencies enriched the business narrative with a diverse set of capabilities and shared excitement.

The agencies were more than just collaborators; they became key storytellers, adding new chapters to the evolving storyline.

James maintained these ties with specific organizations in the heart of Commerceville, where the spirit of collaboration thrived. The agencies, no longer just partners, but key contributors, took the "Cash In On Strangers" voyage to new heights.

The event unfolded as a tribute to the power of collaboration, demonstrating the enormous impact of obtaining assistance from specific groups.

And so the chapter began—a story of collective achievement in which teamwork, particularly with agencies, served as a strategic driver for growing the network of "Cash In On Strangers."

The voyage continued, spurred by a combination of different talents and a shared vision, all with the goal of growth and exploration.

The Cool Factor: Discovering Why Every Way is Awesome

"If you don't find a way to make money in your sleep, you'll work until you die" Neil Pate

In the thriving town of Commerceville, James D. Hudson, the mastermind behind "Cash In On Strangers," realized that the numerous tactics for attracting new clients were not only productive, but also cool. As the stories progressed, the reasons why each method was fantastic became clear.

1. Referral Magic: Clients Tell Clients

Why it is cool: It's like a pleasant rippling effect. Clients become storytellers, sharing their great experiences with other clients, who join the adventure. It's a real recommendation that fosters community by connecting people via shared tales.

2. Employee Teamwork: Ambassadors from Within

Why it is cool: The workplace evolves into more than simply an office; it becomes a source of enthusiasm and shared experiences. Clients become advocates, not simply coworkers.

It's like a large family working together to make the journey more than just about business, but also about building a supportive community.

3. Affiliate Adventure: Clients Helping Clients

Why it is cool: Other clients outside the office become active players. Affiliates function similarly to clients helping clients.

Each affiliate contributes a unique perspective to the story, introducing "Cash In On Strangers" to new audiences. It's a ripple effect of excitement that's spreading throughout town.

4. Agency Allies: The Power of Diversity

Why it is cool: Agencies bring a diverse set of skills to the table. Graphic design adds visual appeal, digital marketing strategically disseminates information, and each agency brings its unique expertise.

It's like building a dynamic network in which the business story transforms into a tapestry of diverse abilities and shared excitement.

In the heart of Commerceville, where collaboration and innovation thrive, James celebrated each strategy's cool factor. The goal of "Cash In On Strangers" was not only to gain more clients, but also to create a thriving community of storytellers, ambassadors, clients, and allies. Each contributed to the distinct coolness that defined the business narrative, which continued to unfold with excitement and limitless potential.

Chapter 5: Real-Life Marvels: Revealing the Art of Advertising

*The more informative your advertising, the more persuasive it will be." – **David Ogilvy***

In the bustling streets of Commerceville, James D. Hudson embarked on a new chapter of the "Cash In On Strangers" journey—one that went beyond screens and computers to explore the real-life enchantment of advertising.

James believed that advertising was not limited to the digital sphere; it could thrive in the real world, where interactions were more personal and instantaneous.

As he went out to bring "Cash In On Strangers" to life in real-world settings, the town experienced the wonders of advertising unfold.

Imagine going through Commerceville and coming across a vivid mural depicting businesses changed by the inventiveness of "Cash In On Strangers." Passersby couldn't help but pause and take in the visual story, enthralled by the brilliance that transcended computer screens.

James arranged events that drew attention and generated conversation. Whether it was a pop-up shop displaying the unique techniques of "Cash In On Strangers" or a live presentation in the town square, these real-life experiences left an indelible mark on the community.

Billboards with smart and appealing messages appeared at major junctions, attracting the attention of both locals and visitors.

Each billboard was more than simply an advertisement; it was a work of art, meticulously designed to convey the essence of "Cash In On Strangers."

The power of advertising in real life extends to unexpected places. James turned everyday objects into canvases for creativity, from benches with intriguing slogans to sidewalk chalk painting that encouraged people to interact with the business.

As the municipality embraced the real-life wonders of advertising, James noticed a tangible connection between the community and "Cash In On Strangers".

The plan was more than just increasing awareness; it was also about creating unforgettable experiences that imprinted the brand into the fabric of everyday life.

In the heart of Commerceville, where the streets became a canvas for expression, James relished in the real-world success of advertising.

The chapter unfolded as a monument to the power of combining creativity and the physical world—an exquisite dance that brought "Cash In On Strangers" to life in the eyes and hearts of the community.

As a result, the real-life marvels of advertising formed a different chapter in the ongoing narrative, demonstrating that the enchantment of "Cash In On Strangers" was not limited to pixels and screens, but thrived in the palpable energy of Commerceville's streets.

Beyond Screens: Unveiling Real-Life Adventures

*People don't buy what you do, they buy why you do it. Always remember that." – **Simon Sinek***

In the bustling town of Commerceville, James D. Hudson was on a mission to reimagine the advertising narrative for "Cash In On Strangers."

He believed in the power of reaching out to everyone, not just through computers and devices, but also by infusing the town's streets with the energy of real-life encounters.

As the sun painted the sky in orange and pink, James set his eyes on turning the commonplace into something exceptional.

He saw a world in which "Cash In On Strangers" were not limited to the digital sphere, but also permeated the physical locations where people lived and breathed.

The first brushstroke on this real-life canvas was a mural—a masterwork that graced the wall of a building in the center of Commerceville. The mural featured stories of firms transformed by the imagination of "Cash In On Strangers."

Passersby were riveted, lured into a story that sprang off the page and resonated with the pulse of the town.

But James did not stop there. He wanted Commerceville to have an experience with the brand that exceeded expectations. He organized activities that brought the spirit of "Cash In On Strangers" to life.

A pop-up shop appeared on the town square, displaying the innovative strategies that had become synonymous with the brand.

It was more than simply a shop; it was a living experience, inviting the community to immerse itself in the world of creativity and inquiry.

Billboards were another canvas for James' imagination. These billboards, deliberately placed at crucial junctions, were not only advertisements, but also works of art. Clever and captivating statements drew the attention of both locals and visitors, making a lasting impression on all who walked by.

The metamorphosis of ordinary objects, however, was perhaps the most unusual and charming component of James' real-life advertising adventure.

Benches transformed into storytellers, embellished with statements that piqued interest and captivated people seeking respite.

Sidewalk chalk painting transformed the prosaic sidewalk into a canvas for creativity, enabling people to interact with the brand in unexpected ways.

As the town welcomed this new kind of advertising, James noticed a shift in how people interacted with "Cash In On Strangers."

The plan was more than just visibility; it was about creating memorable moments that established a meaningful link between the business and the community.

In the heart of Commerceville, where streets have become galleries of expression, James celebrated the success of bringing "Cash In On Strangers" to life beyond screens.

The chapter emerged as a demonstration of the power of combining imagination and the physical world—an exquisite dance that transformed the town into a canvas for real-life adventures.

As a result, the real-life debut of "Cash In On Strangers" became a standout chapter in the ongoing saga, demonstrating that the brand's magic was not limited to pixels and screens, but thrived in the palpable energy of Commerceville's streets, where every corner told a story and every interaction became a real-life adventure.

The Blueprint of Brilliance: Developing a Practical Plan

*Always deliver more than expected." – **Larry Page***

In the bustling town of Commerceville, James D. Hudson sat down to connect all of the amazing ideas into a clear, practical plan for "Cash In On Strangers." He envisioned a step-by-step guide that would bring together the many tactics and make the journey more accessible to everyone.

1. Mural Magic:

- Step 1: Choose a prominent building in the town center to host the painting.
- Step 2: Work with a local artist to illustrate the success stories of firms transformed by "Cash In On Strangers."
- Step 3: Host a community celebration to unveil the painting and celebrate the town's creative spirit.

2. Live Experiences:

- Step 1: Create pop-up shops in high-traffic places to showcase services.
- Step 2: Organize live demonstrations in the town square to engage the community with the brand's unique methods.
- Step 3: Document these encounters using images and videos to share online, linking the real and digital worlds.

3. Artistic Billboards:

- Step 1: Determine critical junctions for billboard placement to increase exposure.
- Step 2: Create visually appealing and witty statements that capture the essence of "Cash In On Strangers."
- Step 3: Rotate billboard content on a regular basis to keep it new and attract passersby's attention.

4. Everyday Object Transformation:
- Step 1: Choose strategically located benches for message placement in high-traffic areas.
- Step 2: Use sidewalk chalk to create temporary art projects that offer a sense of surprise and delight.
- Step 3: Encourage community engagement by asking residents to post images of their improved locations on social media.

5. Real-life events:

- Step 1: Organize community events that reflect the brand's values, such as charity drives or workshops.
- Step 2: Collaborate with local companies to improve the community experience and expand outreach.
- Step 3: Use multiple means to document these events and publish them online, perpetuating the real-life narrative.

As James carefully described these phases, he imagined the town pulsating with enthusiasm, with each part adding to the overarching story of "Cash In On Strangers." The practical strategy became a blueprint for brilliance, guiding ideas into actual, impactful experiences.

In the heart of Commerceville, where creativity meets strategy, James gladly discussed the practical plan with his team.

The journey was no longer a collection of fascinating ideas, but rather a planned approach to leaving a lasting imprint on the community. So, equipped with the blueprint of genius, the "Cash In On Strangers" embarked on the next stage of their incredible journey.

Conclusion

In the heart of Commerceville, where creativity and invention danced through the streets, James D. Hudson marveled at the end of the epic adventure documented in "Cash In On Strangers."

The final chapter was more than just an end; it was a triumphant celebration, the result of strategic brilliance and the brand's flawless absorption into the vivid fabric of the community.

As the final pages rolled, James mused on the transforming power of storytelling in marketing. Commerceville, once a blank canvas ready to be painted, now had the vibrant brushstrokes of "Cash In On Strangers."

The climax, like the grand finale of a fascinating concert, made a lasting impression that extended beyond the pages of the book.

The Legacy of Mural

The story started with a vision of a painting on a landmark structure in Commerceville's town center. A previously blank canvas now included success stories of local businesses altered by the imagination of "Cash In On Strangers."

It became a visual marvel, a live example of the impact of strategic marketing on the town's surroundings. The community gathering commemorating its debut was more than just an event; it was a collaborative celebration of Commerceville's creative spirit.

Live experiences imprinted in memory

The story unfolded with the establishment of pop-up stores and live demonstrations, each experience imprinting itself on the collective memory of Commerceville.

These concrete interactions transcended the physical environment, becoming digital artifacts via photographs and videos.

The brand's distinctive tactics had become synonymous with excitement, making a lasting impression on both residents and visitors.

Billboards Speak volumes

Strategically placed billboards become landmarks, catching attention with visually appealing and humorous messaging.

The rotation of these billboards provided a continual refresh, keeping "Cash In On Strangers" current and entertaining. Passersby were attracted to the story, connecting with the brand on a visual and intellectual level.

The billboards evolved into interactive components of the town's daily life, rather than simply advertisements.

Everyday Objects As Messengers

Benches transformed into storytellers, embellished with messages strategically placed in high-traffic places. Sidewalk chalk painting turned ordinary pavements into canvases of surprise and delight.

Everyday objects become messengers of the brand's innovation, increasing community involvement.

Residents immediately shared photos of the restored locales on social media, causing a ripple effect that spread the brand's reach beyond physical spaces.

Real Life Events

Community gatherings based on the brand's ideals become catalysts for unity and goodwill. Collaborations with local businesses established relationships within Commerceville, resulting in a supportive network.

The documentation of these occurrences, which was broadcast through multiple channels, helped to reinforce the real-life story.

Each gathering became a chapter in the continuous saga of "Cash In On Strangers," promoting a sense of belonging that went well beyond individual transactions.

In the last moments of the book, as James viewed the journey from inception to triumph, he found himself reflecting on the substance of the brand's success.

It wasn't only about getting clients; it was also about making connections, creating memories, and being an important part of Commerceville's story.

Practical summary

The book began with the concept of a mural, which represented the transformative impact of "Cash In On Strangers" on local businesses.

Live events, such as pop-up stores and demos, brought the brand's goals to life, engaging the audience both physically and digitally.

Strategically positioned billboards and creatively modified everyday things became interactive pieces that integrated the brand into the fabric of daily life.

Community activities and collaborations with local businesses fostered connections in Commerceville, resulting in a supportive network.

The book stressed the importance of documenting and storytelling in preserving the real-life narrative, treating each occurrence as a chapter in the continuous saga of "Cash In On Strangers."

The practical journey concluded in the insight that great marketing is more than simply methods; it's about telling a story that resonates with the community.

"Cash In On Strangers" had succeeded not only in attracting clients but also in becoming an indelible part of the town's identity—a timeless story of success that continued to emerge with each passing day.

As the book came to a close, Commerceville stood out as a vibrant canvas where the echoes of "Cash In On Strangers" resonated in the hearts of its residents—a testament to the transformative power of storytelling in marketing and the long-lasting impact of a brand seamlessly integrated into the life of a community.